MW00637431

HOW I BECAME
A DISCIPLE OF
BABAJI

by
Marshall Govindan

St. Etienne de Bolton, Quebec

Cover photo: The author in Norway, 1994
Photo by: Christian Paaske

Published by:
BABAJI'S KRIYA YOGA AND PUBLICATIONS, INC.
196 Mountain Road, P.O. Box 90
Eastman, Quebec J0E 1P0
Canada
Telephone: (514) 297-0258, or 1-888-252-9642
Fax: (514) 297-3957
Internet: www.iconn.ca/babaji/
E-mail: babaji@generation.net

Copyright: M. Govindan
ISBN 1-895383-04-8

1st edition: February 1997

Printed in Canada

Canadian Cataloguing in Publicitation Data

Govindan, Marshall
How I became a disciple of Babaji

ISBN 1-895383-04-8

**1. Govindan, Marshall.   2. Babaji.   3. Yoga, Kriya.
4. Spiritual biography.   I. Title.**

BL1175.G69A33 1997   294.5'436   C97-900181-1

....

SATGURU

BABAJI

NAGARAJ

Acknowledgement

The author would like to gratefully acknowledge the support and encouragement from his wife Gaetane Annai Ouellet as well as many students and friends who requested him, on many occasions, to publish this account. It was originally written as an "Epilogue" at the request of the Italian publisher Jackson Libri Ltd., which included it in their Italian translation of "Babaji and the 18 Siddha Kriya Yoga Tradition", published in November 1995. It then appeared as a series of four articles in "Babaji's Kriya Yoga Journal", volume 2, numbers 2-4 and volume 3, number 1, in 1995 and 1996. It is currently being published as an Epilogue in the Japanese, Russian, Telegu and Spanish editions of this same work.

Introduction

The author is frequently asked how he learned Babaji's Kriya Yoga. It is a difficult question to answer, because it has not been an easy path. There is a tendency for autobiographies in the spiritual dimension of life to present only wonderful experiences. Their authors do not want to present the difficulties of the spiritual path, lest potential readers become discouraged. It might also affect booksales negatively! Also, rather than nurture the memories of the past, a person on the spiritual path is advised to let go of them. One finds peace and joy in the present moment.

However, when seekers of truth read only of the brighter side of life in such accounts, and subsequently their own personal experiences include many "dark nights" and other difficulties, they often give up their efforts. Such aspirants think that they are not fit to continue, or that there is something missing in the teaching.

The following account by the author of his life will therefore serve to illustrate some of the important lessons learned which permitted him to progress. It is not meant to satisfy some personal vanity. It is shared with deep reluctance, and a sense of dedication to expressing the truth. The author has only been able to find the words by writing it in a detached way, using the third person rather than the usual "I", and by avoiding discussion of his personal inner subjective experiences.

The Kriya Yoga tradition is like a tree. The roots of it are the siddhas and rishis who in ancient times developed the powerful techniques or "Kriyas" which lead one to God realization. The trunk of the tree is Satguru Babaji Nagaraj, who preserved these techniques and taught various ones of them to several disciples up to modern times, including Lahiri Mahasaya, V.T. Neelakantan, and this author's teacher, Yogi S.A.A. Ramaiah. Today we can find many branches of this tree, each bearing different kinds of fruit, according to what their adepts were taught and appreciated. The Divine Mother feeds her children differently, according to their needs. Lahiri Mahasaya taught each of his two sons, and various disciples different sets of Kriyas, and their descendants are each teaching only what they learned from their forbearers. Truth seekers should sample, test and compare what each has to offer, treating Kriya Yoga as a science, as well as an art, requiring skill and practice. Scientists are always ready to experiment with new data, and change their conclusions. Kriya Yoga should not be treated as a religion where there is only one "true way". This is the story of how Babaji fed one soul, tested him, and made him his own.

Chapter 1

Early years and idealism:

The author was born in Columbus, Ohio on June 11, 1948, at 1:15 p.m., and was raised from the age of six months in the coastal communities of southern California, including Laguna Beach, Santa Monica and Westchester. The first son of an aerospace engineer and a homemaker, Harry and Jane Hotz who were devout Lutherans, he grew up with faith in God, the work ethic and baseball. He regularly attended Westchester Lutheran Church's Sunday School. He became an Eagle Scout. He took piano lessons for six years and later played bassoon in the school orchestra. Summers were spent surfing and camping in the Sierras.

During the 1960's fresh cultural currents swept through his life. At the age of 15 he had his first mystical experience during a weekend retreat with classmates. After sharing with them for hours in guided discussions, he suddenly went into a trance in which he saw that there was only One Being in the room, speaking through thirty-five individuals. During the months that followed he began seeking ways to relive this experience through meditation, and reading everything he could find on Zen. He seriously considered entering a Zen monastery in Japan. He decided, however, that he should first learn all that he could about Western traditions and those of other cultures.

He was also inspired by the ideal of public service held out by John F. Kennedy and continued to nurture a life long interest in world affairs. Aspiring for a career in the diplomatic service lead him to take a cross country Greyhound bus trip to Washington D.C. in the summer of 1964 to visit the nation's capital and the School of Foreign Service at Georgetown University. The following year he applied and was accepted by this institution. He began his studies there in the summer of 1966. His classmates included the sons and daughters of diplomats, elite Catholic families from both Americas, and a young man named Bill Clinton.

During the first two years, the conservative culture of Georgetown University, with its coat and tie dress code and Jesuit professors began to conflict with the counterculture and anti-war demonstrations which was growing up around it. He had come to Washington filled with idealism and a strong desire to serve his country in the United States Foreign Service. His roommate and best friend was Christopher Hyland, from Marblehead, Massachussetts, who became something of a mentor for him and introduced him to many celebrities in Washington's diplomatic and political circles. With Chris and Turki Faisal, one of the prominent sons of Saudi Arabia's King Faisal, as well as Talal Shubeilat, the son of the Ambassador from Jordan, he helped to organize the 1967 United Nations Palestinian Refugee Ball in Washington. He dated Chris's friend Dorsey Cabot Lodge, a local student at Marymount College, who was the daughter of Henry Cabot Lodge II, the candidate for Vice-President during the 1960 election, and grand daughter of one of its most powerful Congressional Speakers, Henry Cabot Lodge I. Chris's father, Samuel, had been Henry's first political campaign manager when he ran for Congress in the 1930's and was a trusted adviser to John F. Kennedy during his tenure as President. The author attended the Georgetown University Polo matches and glamourous embassy parties. At the same time, high school friends were returning from Viet Nam in body bags, and sending him letters about the horrors of the war. As the war began to have a personal impact on him he confronted Congressmen who came to speak in defense of it at the University. During the 1967 summer break, back in southern California, he learned more about the counter-cultural values from old high school friends who had been to Haight-Ashbury, and from girlfriends who introduced him to the music and discos of Hollywood.

Disillusionment

When Chris's close friend from high school in Switzerland was jailed for possession of a large quantity of hashish in the deep south, the author became drawn into a prolonged effort to free him. Christopher attended New York City's premier debutante ball in 1967. While seated at a table with his father, Samuel, an important Republican Party figure, and Richard Nixon, he was informed by a high school classmate that their friend, who will be referred to as "Blake", was in jail in a southern prison camp. We will explain the reason for not revealing "Blake's" identity, later on. "Blake" was the heir to one of America's oldest and richest families, with two United States presidents as ancestors. He had recently been featured as one of America's most eligible young bachelor. Chris and Blake had together attended the prestigious secondary school, Ecole Nouvelle de la Suisse Romaine. Blake's grandfather had stipulated in his will, before he died, that if Blake ever did anything to disgrace the family prior to his 21st birthday, he was to forfeit his inheritance of more than 30 million dollars. A friend of Blake's persuaded him to transport in his car a large quantity of hashish which this friend had smuggled back into the United States. After a traffic accident, the police discovered it in his car and arrested him. Some greedy family members saw this as an opportunity to grab the inheritance for themselves. So when the case came to trial, they lobbied the judge to impose a stiff sentence. He was sentenced to 20 years at hard labor in a notorious prison work camp. He lost his inheritance when rival family members claimed that as a convicted felon he had dishonored the family and so forfeited his right to the inheritance.

Christopher decided to try to visit "Blake" in prison, and to his surprise, succeeded. He made several trips to the prison camp during the fall of 1967 and winter of 1967 to 1968. A Mafia crime family had learned about "Blake's" imprisonment and decided to blackmail "Blake's" family for the inheritance. They threatened to send the photographs of Blake in prison to the newspapers unless they were paid millions from the inheritance fund. "Blake's" family refused their demands for money. The Mafia then decided to apply more pressure upon the family by threatening to publish lurid photographs of Blake in prison after bribing the prison officials to inject him repeatedly with animal hormones and silicon, which made him resemble a very muscular, hairy animal. They also had many erotic tatoos put on parts of his body. For some reason, Christopher was allowed to visit "Blake", perhaps because, the extortionists thought that he might also be able to put pressure upon the family. As "Blake's" appearance was gradually transformed, after each visit, Christoper came back with more tales of horror. He confided this only with his father, Samuel, and his best friend, the author. His father, who had fought the Mafia as a public prosecutor and prominent Boston attorney years ago, advised him not to get involved. But he had to try to rescue his friend. So together with the author, several courses of action were taken.

First of all, they went to the Federal Bureau of Investigation. The officials told them that by the time they could act upon a federal search warrant, "Blake" would be disposed of by the prison officials. There had recently been reports of similar corruption as well as murders by prison officials in several southern prison camps. Nor did they have the manpower to try to save one unfortunate prisoner in the face of more pressing duties.

Chris and Blake also approached a United States senator who happened to be a relative of "Blake". He refused to make any effort to help.

Finally, they contacted Vito Genovese, whose father, also named "Vito Genovese" was the head of the largest Mafia crime family in America and then serving a sentence in Leavenworth Prison. Vito II had been the resident of the room next door to the author in the Georgetown University dormitory during their freshman year. The roommate of Vito II, was the son of the Mafia's chief money launderer and lawyer. Chris and the author asked Vito II and his roommate to find out whether there was anyway the Mafia could be persuaded to stop this campaign of blackmail. The report came back that since it was being conducted by a different family from the Genovese family, their was nothing they could do to interfere.

Chapter 2

A Search for Meaning:

This affair profoundly disturbed and depressed the author. Frustrated by an inability to help "Blake", the author decided to leave Washington during his third year, and to participate in a program sponsored by Georgetown University at the University of Fribourg, in Switzerland, beginning in September or 1968.

While touring Europe alone in a Volkswagen during the summer before the school term, he picked up a young Englishman hitchhiking in southern France, who invited him to his mother's vacation home in Cadaquès, Spain on the northern Mediterranean coast. A family friend was Salvador Dali, and the author was invited to Dali's home on several occasions over a two week period. Dali and his wife Galla had a magical effect on him and he began to see the world in a new light. A house guest of Dali, Philip Wellman, was creating psychedelic art for Dali. Philip and the author became friends. Over the next four months they were inseparable. They drove to Marrakech, Morocco and then back to Paris and London together. They installed the first psychedelic light machines in the discotheques of Paris. In the summer and fall of 1968, in Paris, they made a lot of money, had a Rolls Royce and moved with a swinging crowd of young starlets, fashion photographers and film directors who were experimenting with psychedelic drugs. However, when he was threatened with expulsion from the University because of his absence, he was forced to choose between studies in Switzerland or becoming a draft-dodging expatriate psychedelic entrepreneur. He struggled with the decision. There was an overwhelming desire to understand recent experiences and to heal his existential crisis. He was finally persuaded that the peace and quiet of Switzerland would help him to sort things out.

During the next year while a resident of the Foyer St. Justin, a student dormitory in Fribourg, he wrote a novel based upon his recent experiences beginning with his experience with "Blake's" case in Washington. He completed it a week after his return to his family's West Los Angeles home. Writing enabled him to "get it out of his system". Upon the eve of his departure, in the Cafe Flore of Paris, at a 21st birthday party his friends gave him, he announced that "with them he had finished doing everything he had wanted to do in life" and "had nothing more to do in America". Only the threat of the draft compelled him to return.

The discovery of Kriya Yoga:

However, during the first week of his return, at the invitation of a friend of his younger sister Gail, named John Probe, he visited the Self Realization Fellowship's Lake Shrine in Malibu. It had been founded by Paramahansa Yogananda in 1952. He read Yogananda's *The Autobiography of a Yogi* and found the answers to many existential questions he had been carrying for years. He also discovered the existence of Babaji, for whom he felt a particular attraction. It felt like he'd found "home". Thirsting for God realization, he applied for admission into the order of monks of the Self-Realization Fellowship, but was asked by them to wait for one year to make sure that this was truly his calling. So, he decided to spend it completing his final year at Georgetown University. Lacking interest in studies he spent hours plunged in meditation.

Upon his return to Georgetown in September of 1969 the author renewed his friendship with Chris Hyland. He recounted to Chris what had happened to him in the past year, including the novel that he had written. They promised one another never to reveal the identity of "Blake" nor his family, for fear of reprisal which could put both their lives in danger. The author also recounted how he had new meaning in life through Kriya Yoga. Chris told him that he too, had gotten involved in a spiritual group of a different sort, one involved in black magic, during a vacation in the Carribean. He had been promised great political power, which would come after many years, and mentioned that John F. Kennedy had made such a pact as a young man during a visit to the Carribean before the war. Chris told the author that he had been told that he was to draw into their fold a close friend who was currently getting involved in spiritual life, and that he realized now that this person was the author. He persuaded the author to participate in several sessions with him, during which strange psychic phenomena manifested and he was filled with fear and dread. The author participated hoping that he could somehow draw Chris out from under the influence of the dark forces. However, the author became confused as to what was "black" and what was "white", "evil" and "divine" as his involvement with Chris grew.

He finally sought the advice of Father Thomas O. King, S.J., the Jesuit priest who had served as the dormitory floor counselor during his freshman year. He had previously discussed with Father King his recent involvement in yoga, and had learned that Father King had read *The Autobiography of a Yogi*, and had himself participated in yoga retreats with Tibetan monks. While a freshman, he had learned that Father King had once performed an exorcism of a patient, a young man, who had been in the Georgetown University Hospital psychiatric ward. After several years of fruitless treatment, the attendant psychiatrists decided that the young patient was probably possessed, and called in Father King, who had been trained in the Church's procedures for exorcism. During the next few years Father King learned the names of the demons who were possessing the young patient, in order to be able to summons them during the planned exorcism. To do so, he would sometimes burst into the boy's room late at night. After learning the names of all thirteen demons, he performed the prescribed ceremony of exorcism successfully. Father King nearly lost his own life during the ceremony, however, when the demons attempted to take possession of him. (By coincidence, the bestselling book "The Exorcist", by Peter Blatty, was written several years later, and a film, based upon it, was made at Georgetown Universtiy.) The author had gone on a weekend retreat with Father King and had taken his course, "Exploration into Spirit". He had grown to respect him for his wide knowledge of the world's spiritual traditions and so valued his opinion on a vital question: "Are the teachings of Yogananda and Kriya Yoga a path to God realization or a path to the devil?" After recounting to Father King the recent events with Chris, he asked him this question, and received his assurances that Kriya Yoga and Yogananda's teachings were divine. Shortly thereafter, he broke off his relationship with Chris. They were to have no further contact until 21 years later when they met in New York. Chris had become a successful businessman, but was not involved in politics.

As a sequel to Blake's ordeal, while the author was in Europe, with the help of a team of hired commandos, Blake's family rescued him from the estate of a multimillionaire in South Africa, to whom he had been sold as a kind of erotic "pet". They brought him back to the family's New England estate where he continues to vegetate, his mind completely gone.

Meeting Yogi Ramaiah

Shortly thereafter, in late 1969, he saw a tiny notice in the "Free Press", a local counter-cultural newspaper in Washington D.C., announcing classes in Kriya Yoga. Thinking that it must be a group of students of Yogananda, he was surprised to learn that Yogi S.A.A. Ramaiah, a direct disciple of Babaji, had started a small center in Washington and was visiting it from New York City every month. Walking into the tiny apartment at 1818 Riggs Place N.W. to meet Yogi Ramaiah the first time, he was struck by the luminosity and peace emanating from him. His skin was the color of red mahogany, and his hair and beard were long and black, with streaks of gray in places. He wore only a white cotton cloth tied round his waist which hanged down to his ankles. His speech was both sweet and powerful. He had so much love and devotion for Babaji. He guided the class participants through 18 postures of "Kriya Hatha Yoga", a meditation, chanting of chants like "Shivaya Nama Om" and "Om Kriya Babaji Nama Aum" or Indian devotional songs. There followed a one and a half hour lecture and one hour question and answer period in which Babaji's life, mission and Kriya Yoga were explained with many references to science and the culture of Tamil Nadu, south India.

During the weeks that followed he learned from Cher Manne, the 19 year old follower who was in charge of the Washington center, many details about the life of Yogi Ramaiah. After several more monthly meetings and lectures with him, the author decided that it would be better to follow a living disciple of the great Himalayan master, and in particular, one who manifested so much love for Him. He was also inspired by his message: practice yoga intensively, work in the world without being attached to it, and serve others. Yogi Ramaiah exemplified this ideal, as a householder yogi and physical therapist.

After trying in vain to get Yogi Ramaiah to indicate to him what he should do with his life (he was still thinking of the monastery, as well as the U.S. Foreign Service, whose written and oral exams he had just passed), the author finally decided to "take the plunge" and not only receive initiation into Kriya Yoga from Yogi Ramaiah in the lower east side of Manhattan in June 1970, but also to join the new ashram he was forming in southern California. While a part of him felt alienated from modern, materialistic, war-mongering American society, another part of him wanted to somehow integrate his yogic spiritual ideals with life in the material world. He also felt that the disciplined way of life required by Yogi Ramaiah of the residents of his centers was just what he needed to curb his tendency to get dispersed in too many directions.

Initiation into Babaji's Kriya Yoga:

Shortly after graduating from Georgetown University in early June 1970, the author went to New York City to receive initiation into "Babaji's Kriya Yoga" from Yogi S.A.A. Ramaiah. It was held in a small ashram, a storefront at 112 East 7th Street, in the lower east side of Manhatten, a block from Tompkins Square. There were about 20 other participants who filled the room. During the early mornings and evening of four consecutive days he learned and practiced the six phases of Kriya Kundalini Pranayama breathing and the seven primary meditation kriyas or techniques. On the following weekend, he participated in a four day "Anthar Kriya Yoga" or spiritual retreat in the same location. He learned more breathing techniques, fasted and observed silence for a day. Then he took his turn chanting "Om Kriya Babaji Nama Aum" with Cher besides the small ceremonial mantra yagna fire, which burned under a makeshift chimney in the middle of the apartment ashram. Before receiving initiation into the "Krishna" and "Babaji" mantras Yogi Ramaiah asked him to pay homage to Yogananda, whom the author had regarded as his guru until recently. He focused on Yogananda mentally, and suddenly felt as though Yogananda was embracing him. He had never felt so close to him as at that point. He asked for and received Yogananda's blessings in serving Babaji and Yogi Ramaiah hereafter. A woman named Shanti Sherman, who participated in the same retreat, and who had lived as a nun in the SRF monastery for three years, later shared with the author that she too had never felt so close to Yogananda as at that moment prior to mantra initiation.

A few days prior to this initiation, the author had received a reply from Brother Mokshananda, of the Self Realization Fellowship, acknowledging receipt of the author's letter in which he informed the SRF of his intention to follow Yogi Ramaiah. Brother Mokshananda (who had come into contact with the SRF some months after the passing of Yogananda) in his letter expressed how valuable and rare was the presence of a living guru.

While in New York the author lived in an apartment dormitory center a couple of blocks away. He became acquainted with the dozen disciples who had dedicated themselves to the practice of Kriya Yoga during the previous year. They formed the foundation of his fledging movement in North America. In the previous months some of the disciples had been posted to new centers on the east coast, and two were to soon go to India to reside at his Madras ashram. The author was inspired by their dedication and devotion.

The Kriya Yoga center residency requirements

During the initiation week in New York, after the author had decided to dedicate his life to Kriya Yoga, he had an interview with Yogi Ramaiah about the requirements for living in a Kriya Yoga center. He was asked by Yogi Ramaiah to keep to the ideals of his yoga center residents while living on his own for three months. This trial period would ensure this way of life was truly his. Yogi Ramaiah called his centers "Kriya Yoga dormitories", and by 1970 he had started centers in Manhattan, New York, New Brunswig, New Jersey, Baltimore, Maryland, Washington, D.C. and Montreal, Quebec. Each center had one to three residents. He was asked to put up on the wall of his rented room on MacArthur Blvd, a typewritten document containing the long list of "Rules and Regulations" of the Kriya Yoga Dormitories. These included the following requirements:

1. **Diet:**
   vegetarian, including food which would provide the five tastes in every meal: sweet, sour, salt, hot and astringent;

2. **Fasting:**
   one day per week on liquids, ending the fast with either fruits in season, or on alternate weeks with saltless food

3. **Silence:**
   one day per week, at least 24 hours without-speaking, preferably on the weekend;

4. **Family life:**
   one had to maintain celibacy until and unless one found a life partner who would make Kriya Yoga the basis of his or her life;

5. **"Sadhana" (discipline in remembrance of God):**
   eight hours per day of yoga practice on the average, including the following five categories of practices: (1) postures, (2) the techniques of breathing, (3) the techniques of meditation, (4) mantras or sacred syllables and (5) "bhakti", or devotional activities involving that aspect(s) of God to whom one was most attracted; practice of these various kinds of yoga according to the fol-

lowing schedule: 3 a.m. to 6 a.m.: postures and techniques of breathing and meditation; 12 noon to 1 p.m.: meditation and mantras; 3 p.m. to 4 p.m. meditation; 6 p.m. to 8 p.m.: practice of all five phases of Kriya Yoga indicated above; 11:45 p.m. to 12:45 a.m.: meditation and mantras. If one could not do part of this because of employment, one had to make up the time at another period during the day;

6. **Work:**
an average of 40 hours per week; one could substitute part of it for time spent at school if one was enrolled;

7. **Financial obligations:**
residents were responsible for contributing certain amounts to a rent fund, a food fund and a Kriya Yoga development fund every month. There were also frequent appeals for additional contributions for special projects, including the acquisition of property in place of rental apartments, and the travel and telephone expenses of Yogi Ramaiah.

8. **Dress code:**
one was required to wear only Indian white cotton waistcloths ("dhotis") in the case of men residents. White cotton saris were worn by women residents. On the job, Western clothes could be worn. However, preference was to be given to white clothes.

9. **Growth of hair:**
residents were not allowed to cut their hair; in the case of men this included their beards; in the case of women this included the hair on the legs and elsewhere. The hair was to be worn tied up in a roll on top of the head except at one's place of employment.

10. Visitors:
the main purpose of the centers was to provide an ideal environment where residents could practice yoga for many hours per day without distraction, so visitors were not allowed except during the weekly public introductory classes and up to fifteen minutes thereafter.

11. Social code:
residents were to limit their communication with persons of the opposite sex to that required by their employment, the public yoga classes and the needs of maintaining the centers. This was a reflection of the Indian social code, where even among married couples, men mix only with men and women only with women. The purpose was to avoid unnecessary distractions from the practice of yoga.

12. "Obedience is greater than argument":
this saying and the others which follow were to be posted on a large board on the wall, and reflected upon. One was to be ready to be sent to any part of the world at any time at the direction of Yogi Ramaiah to start a center or to take over an existing one. One was to be prepared to follow the instructions of Yogi Ramaiah without debate.

13. "Simple living and high thinking":
furniture, aside from appliances and chests of drawers and shelving was not allowed in the center. Residents were required to sleep only on the floor and to take their meals while sitting on the floor, eating only with the fingers, to help prepare them for living in India. For the same reason, water rather than toilet paper was to be used to clean oneself after bowel movements. In order to avoid distraction, no televsion or radios were allowed in the centers either.

14."Cleanliness is next to Godliness":
    one was required to avoid the use of soap, using
    ground mung beans instead. The residue of soap
    fills the pores of the skin, blocking the move-
    ment of pranic energy and well as the elimination
    of waste products through the skin. A sesame oil
    bath was to be taken at least once per week.

15. Written reports:
    a daily written record was to be maintained and
    a summary weekly reports were to be sent
    monthly to Yogi Ramaiah regarding: how much
    time had been devoted to various practices of
    yoga during the designated periods and on the
    average per day, how far one had gone in fulfilling
    ones obligations regarding work, financial con-
    tributions, diet, and silence.

A part of the author was inspired by the ideals
embodied in these rules, but a part was also overwhelmed by doubts as to whether he could live up to
them. The encouragement of Cher Manne was crucial at
the beginning. She was so strong in her dedication. They
became very close, and the author felt that he could not
continue in Kriya Yoga without her. Yogi Ramaiah had
repeatedly said that the householder was the ideal in the
Kriya Yoga tradition and encouraged his students to find
life partners with whom Kriya Yoga would be the basis of
his or her life. Most of the students living in his centers
were so paired. Some already had young children or were
expectant parents. The author asked Cher to become his
partner. She accepted on the condition that he first take
the formal vows of dedication to the ideals of center residents expressed above. Yogi Ramaiah gave his blessings
on the proposal but he wanted the author to first live in
the New Jersey center he had established for single men.
The author appealed to Yogi Ramaiah to allow him to
remain near Cher in Washington D.C. Yogi Ramaiah finally agreed to this, though a bit reluctantly.

Chapter 3

Dedication to Babaji and His Kriya Yoga:

During the summer of 1970 the author gradually adapted himself to the rules and ideals of Kriya Yoga while living in a room rented out by a widow on MacArthur Boulevard. He worked fulltime as a clerk in the Saville Bookstore for $2 per hour. He usually shared dinner with Cher and another center resident, Donna, at their center. In September, as planned, they transported Yogi Ramaiah's entire library of 3,000 books and themselves in a borrowed "drive away" car across the country to Downey, in southern California. When Yogi Ramaiah arrived a couple of days later from India, together with another couple, Ronald Stevenson and Ann Evans, they participated in his first California public Kriya Yoga class in a rented apartment. The author's parents attended, and they brought along their veteran Lutheran minister, Reverend Halvorsen. They sat at the back in polite silence during the entire class, but then afterwards, outside, used all of the reasons they could think of to try to persuade the author not to go ahead with his plans to join the Kriya Yoga center. When no argument had any effect, his father said he was so angry that he could have thrown a kitchen sink onto the author. His parents had just invested heavily in his education. While they had never imposed any conditions upon him with regards to a career choice, they were in a state of profound shock that their beloved son was apparently throwing away a promising career in the diplomatic service, in order to join what they considered to be a cult. The author was pained by their confusion and sorrow, and tried to explain to them the merits of the new way of life he was embracing. Until going to Europe two years earlier, he had always remained close to his parents, and had communicated with them frequently. But the author and his parents were just too far apart in their thinking. When he walked back inside the center, he felt shaken. Yogi Ramaiah said, "Well, make up your mind". That was it. The author replied: "I want to join the dormitory and dedicate myself to Babaji and his Kriya Yoga". That night, he recited the pledge of surrender and dedication to Babaji, in front of a lighted oil lamp, and in the presence of Yogi Ramaiah, his American life partner Avvai, Cher, as well as Ronald and Anne. He felt truly blessed and that night, and slept with Cher for the first time.

Early Difficult Lessons:

One of Yogi Ramaiah's first teachings was "get a job". This was an important rule during a period when many young people who came to him were dropping out of society, not looking for a way to integrate into it. In many cases, including the author's, the teaching had to be further explained with "grab the first job you can and aspire for something better". Having just graduated from a prestigious university the author had certain notions about what work he should be doing. Most of the possible areas of work however, became closed to him when he showed up for an interview with long hair and a beard. This was during a period when long hair was associated with hippies and drugs. Society was divided between "us" and "them" and he was one of "them" to members of the other camp. After several weeks of fruitless job hunting from morning to night, the author was getting frustrated. When he'd return to the center empty handed each night, he'd be greeted by Yogi Ramaiah with a question: "Did you find a job?" When the author would give him the news that he had not, Yogiyar would then invariably tell him that he was not trying hard enough. Finally, the author was ready to do anything. He tried going door to door selling encylopedias for a day before he realized that that was not going to work. Finally, he managed to land a job driving a delivery truck for an automobile parts supply store. It was located a few miles from his parents home in Westchester, and clear across town from Downey. It lasted for a few weeks only, then he was laid off. He got another job working for a small import company, typing brokerage documents for a couple of months. Finally, he was called for an interview by the Civil Service Commission. He had taken the examinations shortly after arriving in California. The author got hired as an assistant caseworker for the Department of Welfare, at the Long Beach office, working with families with dependent children. It enabled the him to start paying some of his share of the expenses.

Living with "Yogiyar", as we affectionately referred to Yogi Ramaiah, was intense. In addition to working a full time job, the author had to practice yoga an average of eight hours per day, and spend a lot of time working on special projects, like the organization of the 16th Annual Parliament of World Religions and Yoga at the University of California (U.C.L.A.). He had to contact many guest speakers representing various religious and spiritual traditions. He gradually got used to wearing Indian yogic dress when he went out, despite the occasional catcalls from rednecks on the street or in shopping centers. He wanted to receive the "Advanced Dormitory Training" which consisted of the balance of the 144 Kriyas or techniques. Yogi Ramaiah had promised to teach the 144 Kriyas to those persons living in the centers who had fulfilled a number of conditions by the end of 1970. These conditions included doing an average of eight hours of yoga per day, every week for six months. Fulfilling all of the conditions was taxing and at times, the author felt discouraged and moody. Cher, in contrast, was strong and steady. She had difficulty in accepting his vacillating nature and doubts. They quarreled at times, and on several occasions sought and received Yogiyar's wise counsel in improving their relationship.

In late January 1971, Yogiyar met with both Cher and the author together and informed them that despite all of the efforts they as a couple had made, the relationship should end, because the genuine love which the author had for Cher was no longer reciprocated by her. If the relationship were to continue, Cher would soon feel forced not only to leave the author, but Kriya Yoga as well. It was painful for the author because of the expectations he had for a long term relationship with Cher. But he wanted Cher to be happy. Yogiyar also held out another route for her as an "ashramite", wherein she would live in close proximity to him, and receive a higher level of training.

Alone in the backyard of the Norwalk center he found himself crying, trying to make sense of her leaving him. Reflecting on what had happened, the author realized that while he sincerely wanted to continue in this path, a part of him found it very difficult to do so, because of some of the rules, like those pertaining to the yogic dress code. He also found it difficult to deal with the pain and resistance of his parents, the financial pressures of not being able to find a decent job, and the lack of sleep at times due to the long hours of "karma yoga". His difficulties had too often been a source of friction in the relationship with Cher. She had helped him to overcome much of his resistance over the past year, and for this he felt eternally grateful. But the effort had taken its toll on the relationship.

With the love he felt for Babaji and the beauty of the Kriya Yoga and the way of life Yogiyar had introduced him to, however, he felt much inspiration. Through Babaji's grace he found the strength to accept her leaving and to look forward to new assignments in Chicago and India.

When it was announced to the other disciples that the "trial" relationship between Cher and the author was ending, it was also announced that the author was to be sent to Chicago, after the Advanced Dormitory Training was completed in the spring of 1971.

Shortly after their relationship ended, Yogiyar also told the author that he had passed a difficult test and that as a result he would go far in this field.

Cher dedicated herself to Kriya Yoga and soon conceived a son "Annamalai" with Yogiyar. They all went to the "kumba mela" at Hardwar in 1974, and later to Badrinath. However, shortly thereafter, she dropped out of the ashram. Yogiyar was kind enough to show the author the letter she wrote in departing. In it she expressed her gratitude for all that she had received and her admiration for Yogiyar, but that she could no longer continue to live the disciplined way of life which he required.

The First Assignments:

In April 1971, after completing the 11 weeks of training in the Advanced Dormitory techniques, Yogi Ramaiah sent the author to Chicago to start a Kriya Yoga dormitory. He drove his old van across country and found a 1 1/2 room apartment in the 2800 block of Orchard Street. He got a job working in a warehouse loading by hand heavy crates onto tractor trailer trucks for $2 per hour. He drove a taxi for Evanston Cab Company at night. In the fall he got a new day job working as a a social worker with the Cook County Department of Welfare in a rough neighborhood close to the skidrow section of downtown Chicago. He started giving weekly public yoga classes, and began practicing the 144 Kriyas intensively. On Sundays, he did "tapas", non-stop meditation for at least 24 hours. He worked hard. Yogiyar had asked him to save $5,000 for a one year assignment in India starting in August 1972.

The great day of his departure for India finally came. He was filled with anticipation, as his predecessors there had all met with disasters. David Mann, who met him at the airport had spent the previous six months in bed with jaundice. David had all of his money and papers stolen; David's predecessors, a couple, Dolf Shriffen and Barbara Lintner, had quit the ashram a month after Yogiyar had left them in charge. Dolf wound up in a mental asylum in Bangalore. Barbara was left completely stressed out in her period of pregnancy.

During the first week, when David showed him around Madras and made him familiar with his duties in the ashram, he felt a lot of insecurity, knowing that in a few days David would be leaving him alone in India. Just after he said goodbye to David at the airport and returned to the ashram by the seashore in San Thome, Madras, he fell sick with diarrhea and fever. After a few days, he realized that it was due to the buttermilk which he was buying in the shop. He stopped taking it and limited himself to boiled water.

During the next nine months the author divided his time between the ashrams in San Thome and Kanadukathan, the ancestral village of Yogi Ramaiah. To get to the latter, he had to take an express bus, which took about eight hours, or a train which took even longer. He gave yoga asana classes in both places as well as in some local temples every week. Such yoga classes consisted of the 18 postures, chanting and devotional songs, done on the verandah of the ashrams. Sitting on grass mats in the hot, humid evenings the classes were attended mostly by local children and an occasional adult. It was a great joy to interact with these children as they were so playful. Many of them, however, seemed to be more interested in getting a piece of sugar candy at the end of the class, than in doing the postures. The Tamil day is punctuated with events which involve interacting with the various forms of God. Prayers and offerings of food or drink are always present, and one receives "prasad", or food which has been offered and blessed by God, in return. Often the priest who was responsible for the temple arrived during the yoga class, and the yoga students stopped and participated in the worship ceremony. Someone rang the large temple bell, and everyone chanted the refrain to the priest's devotional song, standing in rapture as he waved the camphor lamp before the stone and silver images of Ganesha, Shiva or Muruga.

Every day, one of the author's duties was to distribute glasses of buttermilk to the poor in the local neighborhoods. The children would clamor around him to get their buttermilk. He would also feed an "appalam" or large lentil wafer to the crow who came every morning.

There were numerous administrative tasks as well. These tasks involved the maintenance of the ashrams, accounting, taxes, supervision of servants, book publication, shipping of special items including granite sculptures back to North America for use in temples.

The author also visited regularly the birthplace of Babaji, a triangular parcel of land belonging to the central government's customs department, in the seaside village of Porto Novo. To get to it he had to take a horse drawn cart from the train station. He slept out under the stars, among the thorn bushes, dreaming of the time when, nearly two thousand years earlier, Babaji had played there as a young boy.

The author had a lot of time for practicing yoga. He enjoyed doing so, in particular, at Kanadukathan, which was very peaceful and quiet, in comparison to the bustling city of Madras. He liked to go to the Kali temple on the outskirts of the town during the midnight hour and plunge into meditation, ignoring the danger of cobras and scorpions which came out to feed at night. Under the stars at night, practicing the samadhi kriyas, he experienced new breathless levels of awareness and being.

The Kanadukathan ashram was a large house, with a central courtyard upon which all of the rooms faced. The sloping roofs were made of red clay tile, which resembled those of his native California. The walls were made of brick, and were three feet thick to insulate them from the heat. Rooms were used only for storage. He lived on the interior porches which faced the central courtyard. A large room at the rear served as the kitchen. Holes in a low step against the back wall served as the stoves. Branches of wood were shoved into their side openings, and the smoke escaped out of the windows above them. Huge rats, larger than cats, roamed about at night. Sometimes he and his servant boy, Lakshaman confronted these rats with large wooden sticks.

The ashram facilities were very rudimentary. The author slept on the concrete floor on a mat, covered only by a lightweight cloth. The cloth helped to protect him from the mosquitoes, without adding to the discomfort of the hot steamy nights. He also ate while sitting on the floor, using a banana leaf as a plate. After finishing eating, it was easy to simply roll the leaf up and toss it out the window to a spot where the cows or goats would consume it. His meals were prepared by a servant cook, a young mother of three small children. The cook came every morning with dried cow dung to burn in the earthen stove of our kitchen. During the day, she gathered cow dung in the lanes of the small village of Kanadukathan. For breakfast she prepared rice cakes, known as "iddlis" or rice pancakes, known as "dosai", along with a curry spiced with coriander and tamarind, as well as small, deep-fried lentil donuts, known as "vadai", and a small cup of boiled milk and honey. Lunch consisted of white rice, cooked in an earthen pot, a lentil curry and stir fried vegetables, including cabbage, eggplant, tomatoes, plantain or green beans, as well as buttermilk. Dinner was usually a light meal, perhaps a "dosai" or some porridge.

To bathe, the author had to pull up buckets of water from a 15 foot deep well in the back garden and pour it over himself. Ground mung beans and sesame oil were used during the bath at least once per day, but bucket showers were taken to cool off three or four times a day when time permitted.

To wash his clothes, he used the Indian method, which consisted of rolling up soap and water soaked clothes on a flat rock and squeezing or slapping them against the rock to force out the dirt. The wet clothes were swung over the shoulder and down onto the rock with as much force as possible. Then they were dipped in a bucket with a "blue" powder and hung out to dry on a bush. As his clothes consisted of only a "dhoti" (a large sheet worn from the waist to the ankles), a "tondrue", (another smaller sheet draped around the shoulders) and a "kaupin" (loincloth), doing the laundry, was vigorous, but not complicated.

The only amenity was a Western style toilet installed in an outhouse in the rear garden. Toilet paper being non-existant, he'd learned to clean himself after using the toilet in the traditional manner with a mug of water rather than toilet paper.

Once a week the author would travel to the small town of Karaikudi, 12 miles away, to shop for food in the outdoor market. Everything was bargained over, and brought back in cloth shoulder bags. It took all day to travel back and forth on the rugged country buses. He gave a yoga class the Ganesha temple in Karaikudi in the evening during this weekly trip. He would return home late at night. Walking from the bus stop to the ashram under the wide star-lit skies, passing banyan trees, village water reservoirs, goats and barking dogs. The nights were unforgettable. At night the electric power was usually not available so he learned to live by the light of oil lamps, candles and flashlights.

Before coming to India, Yogi Ramaiah made the disciples live like Indians, eating while sitting on the floor, using one's fingers rather than forks and spoons, cleaning with water rather than toilet paper, wearing Indian clothes, boiling drinking water, and eating spicy Indian food. This preparation made the transition easier. It has also instilled within him a preference for "simple living and high thinking". In the pursuit of creature comforts in the West, and increasingly even in India nowadays, people often lose sight of their true source of lasting joy, which is found only inside oneself.

In March 1973, along with Edmund Ayyappa, who was to take over the duties of the author, they travelled to New Delhi to try to obtain permission to purchase from the central government the parcel of land where Babaji was born. After meeting with Dr. Karan Singh, the Minister of Tourism, who had befriended Yogi Ramaiah at the holy festival known as the Kumba Mehla in Allahabad in 1971, doors were opened to them, and finally, permission was granted. In 1975, a beautiful granite shrine was constructed on this sacred spot.

Photographs

Chris Hyland,
Georgetown U.

Marshall Govindan building his first
Ashram, 1954

Phill Wellman, "the first
hippie in France"
according to french
television, 1968

Author in Wencelas Square, Prague,
Czechoslovakia, July 1968

The author with Beatriz Margain, daughter of Mexico's ambassador

The author
with his mother, Jane,
at the Acropolis,
Greece, 1968

Yogi S.A.A. Ramaiah
with Avvai Leslie Stella
at Mt. Shasta,
December 1970

Author with
Yogi S.A.A. Ramaiah
in Chicago, 1972

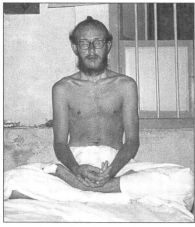

Yogi S.A.A. Ramaiah, 1971
.

The author in San Thome,
Madras Ashram, 1972 (above and below)

Babaji Nagaraj in the San Thome
Madras Ashram, October 1952

Author in Washington D.C., Kriya Yoga Center in 1973

Yogi S.A.A. Ramaiah
1974

Author performing a pooja to a sacred Tulasi plant in Washington D.C. Kriya Yoga Center, 1973

Left to right: The author, Edmund Ayyappa and Yogi Ramaiah in a procession at the start of the 1974 Ayyappa Swami pilgrimage in Imperial, California

Vasudeva Falls
near Badrinath, Himalayas,
1974

Babaji Temple, Washington D.C., 1977

Author with the Katirgama Temple President and Vishnu Murthi, 1980

Katirgama Temple, Sri Lanka, where Murthi of Vishnu is installed

Muruga Temple with "Nandi" bull in Richville, New York in 1979

Muruga Temple chariot during festival, Richville, New York, 1989

Author in
Red Square, Beijing,
China, in 1985

Temple in Kumbakonam,
Tamil Nadu, India

Badrinath Temple, 1987

Babaji and Annai Murthis,
Madras Ashram in 1986

Ramalinga
Rameswar
Temple,
Yuma, Arizona,
1987

Interior view of Yuma Temple, with Murthis of Babaji, Shiva,
the 18 Siddhas and the Ram family

Gopuram Tower over
front gate of
Kanadukathan ashram
depicting 18 Siddhas
1986

Yogi Ramaiah with his son
Annamalai, about 1985

Sri Dharmananda Madhava Swamy,
disciple of Bogar Siddhar (pictured
in background) at the Palani
Temple, Tamil Nadu, August 1985

Yogi S.A.A. Ramaiah
in Montreal, 1988

Procession of naked "Nath" sadhus at "Maha Kumba Mela",
Hardwar, 1986

Right to left: Manigurukul, priest of Porto Novo, India, Babaji Temple,
author, Annai, wife of priest, 1990

Physical therapy building at the Babaji Holistic Yoga Hospital,
Athanoor, Tamil Nadu, India, 1986

Physical therapy building under construction, 1986

Babaji's Kriya Yoga Ashram,
St. Etienne de Bolton, Quebec, 1996

Quebec Ashram meeting room

The author (above and below)
with Gaetane Annai
in Paris 1992

Gaetane Annai 1992

Japanese students with author on retreat, 1994

Advanced Training students with author, Quebec Ashram, July 1995

Chapter 4

Into "the heart of darkness"

When the author returned to Chicago in 1973, he was sent by Yogi Ramaiah to Washington, D.C. to take responsibility for the activities of the small center there. He got a job as a clerk with the Federal National Endowment for the Humanities. He was so enthused with his recent experience in India, that he tried to get his employer and the Director of Personnel to allow him to wear his yogic clothes on the job. They politely refused. He took the civil service exams, and did well on them. He received job offers from the Department of Labor and the Chief of Naval Operations in the Pentagon, to work as an economist in military manpower planning. When he went for his job interview at the Pentagon, he noticed a large sign written over a hallway entrance which read: "Enter the wonderful world of surface warfare". He almost turned around and went back. After asking Yogiyar which job offer he should accept, he was dismayed to hear him say "Take the job in the Pentagon".

After having attended all of the big anti-war rallies against the Pentagon the late 1960's, he wondered whether there existed some karmic reason why he had to go and work there. Shortly after graduating from Georgetown University, he had applied for exemption from military service as a divinity student. He wrote to his draft board that the Kriya Yoga center and its requirements were akin to those of a seminary. Yogi Ramaiah, Ed Prus, his room-mate at Georgetown, and the author's father all wrote letters in his support. He was the first, and perhaps the only person in the history to obtain such an exemption as a student of yoga. Now he had to go and work in "the heart of darkness".

He was disheartened during the first few months there. With his long hair and beard, white shirt, white pants, white shoes, blue blazer and tie, he was an odd sight to the veterans of Viet Nam's jungles. He took a lot of breaks and practiced mantras. Yogiyar, during the middle of a public lecture, chided him for "spending too much time at the snack bar eating peanuts" and for not working hard enough. Because of his powers of clairvoyance, not much got by Yogiyar. Yogiyar no longer gave public demonstrations of such powers as he had in the 1950's and 1960's in Sri Lanka and Australia, where he stopped his heart and breathing for prolonged periods while medical doctors monitored him. However, among his close students, he used them discreetly to assist, or to prod them, but "never for my own benefit" as he sometimes related.

In 1975 and 1976, along with a handful of Washington area students, he purchased a house at 6918 6th street N.W. and moved the center there. The author organized the construction of a beautiful temple dedicated to Babaji in its backyard, in addition to organizing the 22nd annual Parliament of World Religions and Yoga at Georgetown University. He worked a second job in an Indian restaurant to save money for the heavy financial commitments. However, everything seemed to crash down around him when Yogiyar "crushed his ego" during the Parliament. Yogiyar had instructed his students not to sign their own name, but only their initials to letters on behalf of their organization "Babaji Yoga Sangam". The reason was to help them avoid developing an ego about their role. However, the author had reasoned that the guest speakers with whom he was meeting and inviting to give presentations at the Parliament would be insulted and confused if only the initials appeared in place of a name on correspondence. Yogiyar also complained of the cold in his room, and that the author had neglected to furnish it with an electric space heater. As a result, Yogiyar condemned the author in front of all of the other students and said that he would never be allowed to bear the title of "President" of any chapter of Babaji Yoga Sangam. This incident was only one of many in which Yogiyar made students confront the worst in themselves: pride, resentment, jealousy, anger, insecurity and lust. One either learned to detach from the surging emotions, or one dropped out. Most students dropped out over the years, including many friends.

Posted to "Siberia"

In 1977, one such friend dropped out, and abandoned the Montreal center. After trying unsuccessfully to have another student immigrate there, Yogiyar asked the author to make every effort to go. After six weeks, he was granted an immigration visa by the Canadian government. His Pentagon job was being shifted to San Diego, and he was commuting between Washington and San Diego, when the new Kriya Yoga assignment came. The Viet Nam war was over and there was even a fledging meditation club in the Pentagon. He'd overcome his feelings of alienation towards the military and even completed a Master's degree in mathematical economics at George Washington University, and was getting interested in the practical applications of his work. The author felt torn, as he was still trying to heal the recent wounds to his ego. He felt like he was being sent to Siberia. In San Diego, he could be close to Yogiyar, at least geographically. Yogiyar was spending most of his time at an ashram in the Imperial Valley, near the border of Mexico and California. He wanted to have more contact with Yogiyar, to serve him in a more intimate way. Prayer and devotion to Babaji helped him to make up his mind, and to move to Montreal.

Finding a job proved to be a long difficult process. When not applying for jobs, he painted all three floors of the local sangam's delapidated triplex apartment building. After two months of searching and walking three miles through a blizzard, he got a job as a data entry clerk. Then a few weeks later he got a job as an economist with Bell Canada running a corporate simulation model. However, his supervisor's boss took a disliking to him and his espousal of vegetarianism. After a year and half at Bell he was asked to look for another job. He promptly found a better one, as a manager of corporate analysis at Teleglobe Canada, the overseas telecommunications carrier.

Every weekend for the next 11 years, with the exception of a year in 1980-81 and 1985-86, the author drove 300 miles roundtrip to Richville, in upstate St. Lawrence County, New York. His duty was to conduct a public asana class there, to which no one came. Actually, one local farmwife, Marlene Nault, and later her husband did start coming during the last few years. They were eventually initiated. More importantly, was his duty to perform a "puja" to Lord Muruga, in the temple which had been built in 1975 on the 30 acre tract of land owned by the New York sangam. The land had been purchased by Yogiyar at an auction, sight unseen, for $3,000, for the purpose of having a place for retreats. The idea for building a temple on a small hilltop there came during one such weeklong retreat in July 1975 when Yogiyar had a dream in which Babaji ordered him to have it completed within the next three days, in time for the initiation into mantras. The 30 odd students worked day and night with a local stone mason to complete the 18 foot high, 13 foot square cinder block structure, topped by a five stepped pyramid of blocks. Granite statues of Muruga and his two goddess shaktis, "Valli" and "Thaivani" were installed inside. A white Charlolais bull calf was purchased to lead the 7 mile pilgrimage to the temple. The pilgrimage was made along the country roads, chanting "Vel Vel Muruga, Vathi vel Muruga" in emulation of the great "water-cutting" ceremony done with an elephant at the Muruga temple in Katirgama, Sri Lanka.

The author also had to take care of the bull calf, which soon grew into an 2,000 pound adult. His name was Nandi. It is illegal in New York to allow a bull to wander freely even behind a fence, so the bull had to be tied to chain which was attached to a 4 foot long stake, which in turn was twisted deeply into the ground with a 5 foot long steel bar. Every week he had to catch the bull by the nose ring and move the stake to a new grazing area. It was a perilous operation. He also had to walk the bull at least a mile to keep him in shape. Nandi was attracted to the cows in their neighbors' fields. He had not been castrated and would try to run away to mate with them. He sometimes broke his chain, or tried to break free when being walked. He was cunning, unpredictable, extremely quick and powerful. If Nandi detected any fear in the author he would strike out with his head or hoofs. On several occasions he got the author down on the ground and tried to crush him with his head. After these incidents the author called Yogiyar and tried to persuade him to find a smaller animal for the annual procession and ceremony. But Yogiyar was adamant. The white bull was the symbol of Shiva's vehicle, and had to stay. The author gradually learned to control his fears through detachment.

Chapter 5

Pilgrimage to Sri Lanka

These were wonderful years, in which the author practiced Kriya Yoga for an average of eight hours a day. He completed more than 50 days of tapas in which Kriya Yoga was practiced for 24 hours without a break. Many wonderful spiritual experiences occurred,particularly in the Richville shrine, as the author became more devotional, and turned inward.

A few weeks every year, during vacations, he went to retreats with Yogiyar at the ashrams in Arizona or California, or to act as Yogiyar's assistant. Yogiyar wore out his personal assistants and rotated them every two weeks. He would keep them so busy that they would only get about two or three hours of sleep per night. During the retreats and classes he would read out a verse from one of the Siddhas. After meditating upon them, he would give a lecture on the meaning of the verse. In this way, students became familiar with the vision and culture of the Siddhas, even though he'd written very little about their teachings. Yogiyar's lectures were inspired. At times, it seemed as though the Siddhas, in particular, Boganathar, spoke through him, especially when he was expounding upon the Siddha's verses. During the retreats, Yogiyar's severe authoritarian, personality was often replaced by a sweet, loving one. During mantra initiation, it seemed to merge with that of Babaji Himself.

In 1980, Yogiyar sent the author back to India. This time there were many pressing projects: the supervision of the printing of the complete writings of the Siddhar Boganathar, the renovation of the Madras ashram, the purchase of a large tract of land which would be the eventual location of a college of yogic therapy and physical therapy, and the building of an ashram in Dehiwala in Sri Lanka. When his visa in India expired, he went to Sri Lanka, a tropical paradise on a large island southeast of the Indian subcontinent. For years the author had heard stories about Sri Lanka, including those related to the famous shrine of Lord Muruga, in the jungle at Katirgama, where Babaji had experience enlightenment under the tutelage of his first guru Siddhar Boganathar.

The author's first stop was Colombo, the capital, on the southwest coast. Afterwards he travelled to the one-room center which had been rented by his predecessor there, Meenakshisunderam. It was at the end of Canal Bank Road, in Dehiwala, just across the small canal separating the Welawatte section of Colombo from Dehiwala. The center was built up against the rear wall of a plantation owner's estate. It was opposite the beach and the Indian ocean, in an isolated section of Dehiwala, a suburb just south of Colombo. He was in for a rude shock when he crossed the threshold. "You'll get used to the rats and their droppings," Meenakshisunderam announced in a matter of fact way as we walked into the dingy room. The author peered through the darkness up at the ceiling and then down at the floor in horror as Meenakshisunderam added, "The rat droppings covering the floor fall from the spaces between the lattice boards up there in the ceiling. The rats have their nests up there."

"I'm not staying here," the author replied with a cry, but he somehow knew that there was little he could do to extricate himself from the situation. He started having flashbacks to the period when he walked into

Meenakshisunderam's roach infested apartment next to
their center in Washington where they lived together in
1973-75. "Which was worse?" he wondered. This dingy
room would be his home for the next nine months.

Meenakshisunderam introduced the author to
Yogiyar's local students at one of their weekly meetings at
the Bambalapitya Hindu High School. There they practiced the 18 postures and chanted devotional songs and
chants on the balcony. Meenakshisunderam departed for
America a few days later. Despite the simplicity of the
author's room, after cleaning it up and visiting the sur-
rounding area, he quickly began to appreciate the beauty
of Sri Lanka, its people and culture. He resolved to
devote himself to some serious sadhana here, but first
there was work to do.

The author had brought with him on the plane from
Madras a 24-inch high 50 pound granite sculpture of
Vishnu, in a standing pose. Yogiyar had given its commission to Ganapathy Stapathi, a well-known sculptor in
the village of Mahaballapuram. This village is famous for
its sculptors and is located just south of Madras. It was to
replace the statue which had been removed by thieves
from the temple. It was situated to the right of the god-
dess-Thaivani-Amman temple at Katirgama. After travel-
ling for an entire day on a bus along the coast and then
through the forest he arrived at the village of Katirgama.
As he approached the temple, carrying his load, he was
overwhelmed by the the vibrations of peace and beatitude emanating from it. He had rarely felt so close to God
as when he approached this temple. He passed through a
large wrought iron gate, flanked on both sides by walls
whose face was carved into a row of sculptured ele-
phants. Their gray heads, white tusks, chests and legs
protruded from the wall majestically. Monkeys clam-
bered on top of the walls. Through the gate he perceived
a row of three single-storey buildings, the temples, sur-
prisingly unremarkable in terms of architecture. Their

roofs consisted of corrugated tin, slanted at about 45 degrees, rising to a peak. A small bell tower stood in front. A handful of persons were seen coming and going from these temples.

Buddhist priests controlled the functioning of the temple to Lord Muruga. It had become recognized even by the Buddhists that a mysterious power could grant its petitioners their requests. Hindu priests living in the monastery to the left of the temples controlled the functioning of the temples of Ganesha and Thaivani. The author was directed to another gate at the far right end of the wall, the entrance to the Hindu Shaivaite monastery associated with the Thaivani Amman temple. He was ushered into a large dimly lit room. Looking down from the large photographs on the walls were the previous abbots of the monastery sitting upon tiger or deers skins. They were extremely thin and ascetic looking, with long beards, matted hair and huge lustrous eyes. The author marvelled at the strength and courage which the abbots' gaze revealed, and the general aura of sanctity in the hall. While he waited for the appearance of the current abbot, Swami Dattaramagiri, he peeked through the doorway into the garden and saw several rows of small white "samadhi" shrines, the final resting place of the abbots and saints associated with the place. Traditionally, Hindus are not buried, except in the case of saints or heads of orders. Enshrined, it is believed that their disciples can more easily contact them "on the other side".

Soon after, the current abbot, an elderly Swami, came in and greeted the author in Tamil and broken English with an easy, relaxed manner. The Swami had been the abbot for only a few years, having served as a priest there before becoming assistant to the previous abbot. The previous abbott headed the monastery for nearly 40 years and was a person of great sanctity. On his deathbed the previous abbot asked this man, a retired householder, to take vows of renunciation, or "sannyas", and to somehow carry on. It had been difficult for him to do so, but out of devotion to his guru, he had somehow to keep the institution going. He was opposed by a faction of Buddhists who were trying to wrest control over the Ganesha and Thaivani temples from the Hindus. The Swami recounted to the author the difficulties he had experienced. Only two months before, a gang of thugs had entered the monastery one night and beaten him and his assistants severely. He spent several days in the hospital, but the psychological scars had not yet healed. The author's heart went out to him when he lamented the fact that there was no one to succeed him as abbot should something happen to him.

Months earlier during a visit by Yogi Ramaiah, the Swami had hinted that he would be deeply grateful if Yogiyar would send to him a worthy successor from among his students. Yogiyar had mentioned this possibility to a couple of them and the author was infatuated with the idea that he might settle down one day in this peaceful oasis. He was not afraid of political opposition, feeling somewhat immune, as a foreigner, from the threats of violence. The spirit of asceticism flowed through him during his years with Yogiyar, and reached a peak during this long visit to Sri Lanka. He was especially imbued with devotion for Lord Muruga.

Just a few feet to the left of the entrance to the monastery gate was the site of the sacred banyen tree under which Babaji had first experienced enlightenment around 215 A.D. Only about 15 years before the author's first visit, a man had cut down the ancient tree. A few days later this same man was found dead, hanging from a tree, a victim of his own hand. Even now the roots of the tree were growing from the wall of the well inside the courtyard of the monastery. The abbot had given permission to Yogiyar to build a small shrine to Babaji just behind the wall inside the gate of the ashram, to commemorate this spot, so sacred to all of Babaji's disciples.

Containing a granite statue of Babaji in lotus pose, the temple priests make a simple offering to it daily, on behalf of devotees of Babaji everywhere.

After refreshments, the abbot directed the author to a room, where he spent the night, with a remarkable number of mosquitoes. At times he wondered whether he would eventually get used to them, should he be given the opportunity to make this his home.

The next day, before attending the early morning pujas at 6 a.m., the author took a bath in the Manickaganga river, a large stream running through a deep ravine to the left of the temple complex. What a refreshing experience! At one point the author floated on his back as its current carried him for more that 100 feet under the protective arch of ancient banyen trees.

Later the author attended pujas in the Ganesha and Thaivani temples conducted by the resident priest. By tradition, the priest hailed from Benares, as did all of the residents of the ashram. Afterwards came the puja in the temple to Lord Muruga. The outer hall where everyone stood was lit by large standing lamps over-flowing with ghee, or clarifed butter. These were filled periodically from bottles brought by devotees. The puja was conducted by a group of Buddhist priests, dressed in white, who were householders. While more than 100 devotees stood with their offering baskets filled with flowers, fruit, bottles of ghee, packets of incense, vib-huti ash and kumkuma red powder, the priests filed into the outer hall, and then behind a large curtain which shielded the inner sanctum. No one, except the priests, has ever seen what lay behind the curtain. But according to tradition, instead of a traditional stone image of the deity, there is a yantra carved into a sheet of metal. The yantra, a geometric mandala, is said to represent Lord Muruga, and to be empowered with his spirit.

Only once per year, during a July ceremony, this carved yantra is removed, placed in a box, and carried in a procession with much fanfare down to the river on the back of an elephant. The "water cutting ceremony" as it is called commemorates the victory of Lord Muruga over the negative forces. The celebration is attended by thousands of devotees who come from all over Sri Lanka, often on foot. During the festival, dozens of devotees of Muruga walk on long beds of white-hot burning embers, in divine trance, under the protection of their Lord. Others carry the *"cauvery"*, which is dozens of slenders spears piercing their skin and supporting an arch of peacock feathers and other decorations. The devotees are immune from pain and injury.

After the prayers of invocation have been recited by the priests, the devotees deposit their offerings into the hands of the priests who are standing on a platform above the crowd in front of the curtain. The priests take the offerings inside, offer them to the deity, and then return a portion of the offering, "prasad", to the devotees.

During the puja the author was filled with the bliss of Lord Muruga. He felt profoundly grateful for having been allowed to come close to Muruga here, after years of devotional activites in the Richville, N.Y. Muruga temple. Sublime peace and love filled the author in the following days. Embued with bliss,the author visited the other places associated with Muruga in the area: the famous caves known as *Chinna Katiragama* where he met Valli, the shepherdess, and the top of Adam's Peak, where the Buddha left his footprints in stone. In the forests around the shrine of Katiragama he came across a few yogis. The spiritual vibrations of this forest rivaled those of the Himalayas. Sitting in meditation at the place where young Babaji Nagaraj attained enlightenment, 1763 years earlier, the author was filled with wonder. He prayed that Babaji would bless His devotees everywhere.

After a few days, because of his duties back in Colombo, the author was obliged to leave this most sacred of places, dear to all inhabitants of Sri Lanka.

Every week for nearly a year, the author lead a public Kriya Hatha yoga class, meditation and chants for Kriya Yoga devotees in two schools: the Bambalapittya Hindu High School on Sunday mornings and the Hindu Ratnawalla Boys School on Saturday mornings. About 15 initiated adults and some of their children attended the first class regularly. Their devotional *"Thevaram"* hymns, composed by the Saivite saint *Manickavasagar* in the 9th century A.D., and sung in Tamil, were very beautiful and spirited.

The rest of the time the author was free to pursue his interest in sadhana. He remained in silence and ignored all forms of distraction, including newspapers, books and magazines for over nine months. He made his peace with the rats in his room though they still managed to eat his food regularly, even though it was kept overnight suspended from the middle of a clothesline, high above the floor.

He practiced all of the 144 Kriyas regularly and grew in continuous awareness. The first few months were difficult, as the mind struggled with not having any source of distraction. Gradually, a profound calm because to pour into his being. During this time, the technique of "yoga nidra" or "conscious sleep" became easy: he became aware of everything around himself whether his body was in the sleep state or not. He enjoyed the company of many animals and birds, and lived on tropical fruit supplemented with a little rice. It was the most wonderful period of his life. Towards the end, when Yogiyar instructed him to leave, he did not want to go. He was concerned that the hard earned peace would be somehow lost if he returned to North America. But Yogiyar insisted, adding that the author had a lot of work to do, in addition to many desires to fulfill.

During this soujourn in Sri Lanka, he took a couple of train trips to Jaffna, the capital of the northern most province of Sri Lanka, and cultural home to the Tamil minority. He stayed in the home of an initiated student, Mr. Gunnerathnam, a retired civil engineer, at 51 Arasady Road, Vannarponnai. It was not far from the temple dedicated to Amma, the Divine mother. During one visit, he attended the car festival at this temple. The huge juggernaut car is pulled around the temple once a year. On it is placed the idol of Divine Mother, so that she may visit all of her devotees outside the confines of the temple. It is pulled very slowly by hundreds of persons throughout the day, with frequent stops. At one point the author went into a deep trance, his gaze transfixed on Her, in the distance. He was unable to move for nearly a half hour, as waves of bliss poured out of Her and through him. It was as if the whole of creation was alive with Her manifestation.

He also taught Kriya Hatha yoga, introduction to meditation and chanting at the Jaffna Hindu Boys College on Sunday mornings. Established by the British colonials years before, it had produced the cream of Sri Lanka leaders in government, including Dr.H.W. Tambiah, Supreme Court Justice, and the president of Lanka Babaji Yoga Sangam, as our organization was known. The boys were disciplined and respectful. They were a joy to be with.

The author's visits to Jaffna came to an end, however, as the guerilla war, waged by the Tamil separatists in the north, prevented further train travel. Later, he learned that many of his students had been brutally massacred in the ethnic riots which swept the country. It is difficult for him to recall this tragedy without feeling a deep sadness.

Chapter 6

A responsibility to initiate others into Kriya

After returning from India in 1981, the author decided to embark on a new career, one which would permit him to move around as new assignments came from Yogiyar. He began a ten year career in computer systems auditing which culminated in his writing two books on the auditing of electronic commerce, which were published by the professional associations of certified public accountants in the USA and Canada.

In 1983, after Yogiyar had a serious heart attack, and underwent heart surgery, he decided to form a "Board of Directors" which would one day take over from him the responsibility for managing International Babaji Yoga Sangam. The directors were announced by Yogiyar at a meeting of his students in Norwalk. The author was not included among the seven Directors. Later that night, Yogiyar took his dog "Devi" for a walk and asked the author to accompany him. Under a street lamp he asked him to sit with him and to write on a piece of paper the following conditions. Then Yogiyar told him that if he could fulfill these conditions, he would be authorized to initiate others into the 144 Kriyas. The conditions included (1) during one "mandala of 48 days during one of the sadhana periods, cry before Babaji's picture seeking his grace to eliminate the ego and unconditionally surrender to Him and develop Love for Him, his Kriya

Yoga and the Kriya Yoga movement; (2) for 6 mandalas of 48 days without a break in each mandala, ring a bell 5 times according to the Dormitory sadhana schedule, and do sadhana for at least five minutes; (3) make a copy of the Advanced Dormitory Training notes, and send them to Yogiyar in Yuma; (4) Sign the paper on which this was written with a drop of blood stating that he would remain faithful to eternity to Babaji, Kriya Yoga and the Kriya Yoga movement; (5) sign a separate note that as early as possible, he would pay $5,000 towards Yogiyar's samadhi shrine; (6) continue to practice the Advanced Dormitory Kriya techniques till the end of his life.

During the next three years, the author gradually fullfilled the conditions. It was very difficult. On many occasions he would get involved in work at the office and forget to observe the sadhana period, or fall asleep and forget to ring the bell before the end of the sadhana period. Then he would have to start the mandala all over again.

The financial commitment was not particularly hard, for he had given virtually all of his earnings over the years to one project or another in Kriya Yoga, whenever there was an appeal for funds. The author's name appeared on many of the mortgages of the Sangam's properties, including Washington, D.C., Chicago, Yuma, Arizona, and Norwalk, California. Having a good job and no dependents, he had learned to save money for assignments in India by "staying out of stores". He bought his clothes at the Salvation Army, ate simply, and economized in every way he could.

The author grew closer to Babaji, chanting and crying before his picture on his personal altar in the Montreal center. For years, whenever he'd been involved in karma yoga assignments, particularly in India, he felt Babaji's guiding hand, removing obstacles, showing him the way through many problems. He had become adept in contacting him in the seventh meditation Kriya. Now that contact became more and more tangible. He felt His loving presence all around him. Finally, he fulfilled all of the conditions. Yogiyar asked him to have his sadhana notebooks verified by a local student, and to simply wait. From time to time, however, he told the author that one day he would go and start his own order.

The Maha Kumba Mehla and Badrinath

In 1985 Yogiyar and the author visited China together. Afterwards, he told the author to return to India to administer the construction of his clinic for the handicapped, and college of yogic and physical therapy, near the Kanadukathan ashram. Yogiyar and 25 Kriya Yoga students were also planning to attend the 48 day Maha Kumba Mehla in Hardwar, in early 1986. Afterwards they would make a pilgrimage to the temple of Badrinath in the upper Himalayas. So Yogiyar told the author to go to Hardwar, where the Ganges comes out of the Himalayan mountains, to make reservations and preparations for the group.

The author decided to try to get a leave of absence without pay from his employer, Montreal Life Insurance Company. He had worked there for four years as its budget manager and internal auditor. Whenever he finished Kriya Yoga assignments in the past, he usually had to start all over again in a completely new field. He had held many different kinds of jobs, and it always seemed like Yogiyar would ask him to leave one job just when he was getting comfortable with it. Before asking his employer for the leave of absence, however, he first offered a coconut in a ceremony to Lord Ganesha in the temple in Richville, N.Y. He asked Ganesha to simply help him fulfill his financial obligations. Then the author wrote a letter to his boss, the Treasurer, explaining the reason for the leave: to administer the construction of a facility for the rehabilitation of handicapped persons in

India. His boss, in turn asked the President, who said "no" to the request, because "he'd be away too long". But after he read the author's letter, the President came to see him in his office. He said: "You write a very convincing letter... and I'd feel like a (expletive) if I said no". "How much is this trip to India going to cost you?" The author replied by giving him a dollar figure. The President replied: "Well, we will take care of that". As tears began to well up in the author's eyes, he asked: "Why are you offering to pay for my expenses. I only asked for a leave without pay". The President replied: "Then you'll have a moral obligation to come back to us". The author accepted his generous offer and thanked him (and Ganesha and Babaji!) profusely.

The magic in this period was just beginning. The author was alone in India, but had the assistance of a few engineers and contractors. For years, they had all dreamed of building such a college. Yogiyar had been healed of bone tuberculosis by Babaji 35 years before. So he treated the handicapped as though they were the Master Himself, with so much tenderness and love. The site was a barren, flat piece of land, reminiscent of Arizona, with a few thorn bushes and no water. It was a daunting task. A well, eight feet wide was dug by hand during the next two months, 30 feet deep, through rock. Meanwhile, a crew of local laborers, mostly women, carried water on their heads from a stream, nearly a mile away, to the construction site, where the cement foundation of several buildings was being poured. There were innumerable difficulties, but through Babaji's grace and guidance they were surmounted. In eight months, eight buildings were completed on the new campus: the school of physical therapy with its exercise gymnasium and treatment rooms; an out-patient clinic; temple to "Palaniandavar" (the form of Muruga at the shrine of Palani"; an auditorium; a printshop building; guest quarters; entrance gate guard house and poor feeding center; storage buildings. The Kanadukathan ashram also was renovated, with a large tower "gopuram" over the front gate, and temples inside, covered with statues of the 18 Siddhas.

At the end of eight months Yogiyar and the Minister of Industries for Tamil Nadu came and presided over the opening ceremonies of the freshly painted facilities. It seemed like a miracle. In previous assignments to India, projects were slowed constantly by bureaucrats' need for bribes, red tape, by lack of funds or by shortages in building material. But now, everything came together on time. Jai Babaji! The author felt that his life's purpose had been fulfilled. Now he hoped to retire in some center and just practice yoga.

The pilgrims from America arrived for the college's opening, and then they all went to Hardwar. Every 12 years there is a huge gathering of renunciants and devotees from all over India in one of four holy towns of northern India: Hardwar, Prayaga, Ujjain and Allahabad. Every 60 years the event is even more important. The gathering last 48 days. It includes a dozen special days during which the principal activity is the taking of ritual baths in the Ganges River. One of these days is particularly auspicious, and more than 12 million persons bathed in turn at a bypass stretch of the river bank known as Harki Pawri. The military controlled the crowds so that everyone could bathe in turn for a few minutes at this sacred place. The author experienced a transcendental state of consciousness when he waded out and immersed himself in the Ganges on that auspicious day in April 1986.

During the Kumba Mehla the pilgrimage party visited many "sadhus", or holy mendicants who had come down from the Himalayas. Their radiant eyes and faces filled everyone with awe and beatitude. The author enjoyed exploring their campsites, searching for those rare gems of humanity, the enlightened ones, whose demeanor and aura set them apart from the others. But everywhere and in everyone he saw greatness. The millions of devotees who camped there all displayed great courtesy and cooperation. The event was an amazing display of civil order, human dignity, peace and love.

After the Kumba Mehla, the Kriya Yoga pilgrimage party travelled by bus for one and a half days to to the sacred temple of Badrinath, in the high Himalayas, 220 miles from Hardwar. It is located in a valley at an altitude of over 10,000 feet, and surrounded on all sides by mountains rising to over 23,000 feet. Babaji's ashram is only 10 miles away, in the no-visitor zone between Tibet (China) and India. The pilgrims bathed in the natural hot springs and then in the Alaknath River, before attending the early morning puja in the great temple dedicated to Lord Vishnu. They were not permitted to visit Saptkund Lake where Babaji's ashram is situated because of the tensions between India and China. But during the all night "mantra yagna" chanting "Om Kriya Babaji Nama Aum" sweetly around a fire, His presence was evident. Their hearts melted with tears of joy and love.

"Go and teach Kriya Yoga to others"

After the pilgrimage to Badrinath and the official opening of the new clinic and educational facilities near Kanadukathan, the author was sent back to Canada. He resumed his post at Montreal Life, but a few months later it was sold and most of its managers and executives were laid off. The author took French classes to improve his ability in the language, completed his certification in the field of computer systems auditing. He got a job working in this capacity for Quebec's largest financial institution, with whom he remained for the next eight years.

In 1987 the author spent a year of his free time organizing the 32nd annual Babaji's Parliament of World Religions and Yoga at the Queen Elizabeth Hotel in

Montreal, which was attended by more than 1,000 persons and more than 25 speakers representing various spiritual traditions. The President of the Sai Baba temple in Montreal, Mrs. Myriam Josza, came to dinner a few months beforehand to discuss with the author the invitation to speak at the Parliament. Later that night she meditated on Sai Baba and asked him whether she should go or not. Her intuition was confirmed when a few hours later she received a telegram from Sai Baba urging her to go, and extending his blessings on the conference.

Afterwards, Yogiyar asked the author to save for a five year assignment in India. After five years he would be able to obtain a permanent resident visa in India. He was excited by this prospect. But he would take a couple of years to save the required $25,000 needed for such a long assignment.

However, when the author accompanied a group of Montreal students to a retreat in the Yuma, Arizona ashram in November 1988, the author found himself caught in between Yogiyar's discipline and their reactions. They were troubled by the severe scolding which Yogiyar gave to another student there, and he felt obliged to speak to Yogiyar about their pained feelings, as diplomatically as he could. Yogiyar listened politely, and defended his scolding as the only way to get through to the student who had erred.

A few weeks later, however, during a visit to Montreal, on the evening before his departure, Yogiyar brought up the subject again and reprimanded the author for questioning his way of doing things as he had in Yuma. He also scolded the author for developing a friendship with a woman who was a new Kriya Yoga initiate, even though for the past two years, he had encouraged the author to find a life partner. From 1971 to 1986 he had advised him to remain as a celibate monk, with no social contact with women. The author had respected this social code scrupulously. Yogiyar said this woman was not a good choice since she already had a boyfriend. The author listened without debate, but that night he wrote to Yogiyar a letter in which he beseeched him to communicate more openly with him and Yogiyar's other students.

That same evening, a few students were invited to "help" (or rather, watch), Yogiyar pack his belongings for his departure for India. One of them brought a friend named Gaetane Ouellet, whom the author had never met before. They were introduced, but he hardly noticed her that evening, though she keenly observed the activities and unfolding drama. The following morning, December 17, Yogiyar told him that he was not interested in having an open dialogue with him, as the author sought. He was dismayed by Yogiyar's attitude, but accepted it like countless other decisions Yogiyar had made over the past 18 years. The Christmas holidays were about to begin and the author was looking forward to spending the following two weeks in silent meditation.

Early Christmas morning, the author slipped into a state of mental silence and breathlessness. Suddenly, he heard a clear voice saying: "It is time for you to go and teach Kriya Yoga to others". He had heard this voice before over the years, at several critical points in his life when he experienced Babaji's presence and guidance. But this time he saw the Master's youthful form sur-rounded by a golden glow. He had not seen such a light since 1975 when near Pike's Peak, Colorado, during a cross country pilgrimage with Yogiyar. He saw Yogiyar dissolve into this light while he was sitting alone in a secluded spot deep in samadhi. Now, waves of love and bliss swept over him as he noted the details of His beau-tiful form. He felt himself dissolved into it, and then experience a great sense of expansion and profound peace.

After this vision, the author remained indoors, plunged in meditation and devotional activities. Master's command implied that he must leave the Sangam as an organization. He had never even dreamed of doing so, since the early 1970's, after he and Cher had separated. He had taken vows of lifetime allegiance to the Sangam and only wanted to serve this institution. All of his friends were in it. He wondered how would Yogiyar react? However, there were two more visits by the Master, during which he told the author that it was time for him to leave and to begin teaching Kriya Yoga to others on his own, outside of the Sangam. Babaji also said that Yogiyar would understand why, though it would not be accepted by some of his brother and sister disciples who would be jealous of him.

At the beginning of the new year, the author telephoned Yogiyar and simply told him that he was leaving, with Master's blessings and guidance. Yogiyar accepted the news gracefully, but not the author's offer to continue to support the Sangam. "Once you leave, you leave" he replied with finality. Then the author wrote a letter to Yogiyar relating to him the details of his vision of the Master, and the new assignment given by the Master, which obliged him to leave. A few days later, he found an apartment and moved out.

A few weeks later, he met Gaetane Ouellet, by chance. She mentioned that she had completed a 40 day Tibetan Buddhist retreat, a few months earlier, where she had shaved her head. The author told her that he was beginning to teach Kriya Yoga, and she said that she would like to be initiated. They exchanged telephone numbers. A couple of weeks later she called him, and they met and began a series of initiation classes. She became his first student. Over the next few months they fell in love, and on July 2, 1990 they were married in an elaborate and traditional Hindu ceremony in the temple of Chidambaram, Tamil Nadu, India where "Dancing Shiva", Lord Nataraja presides.

Shortly after Gaetane's initiation, Mrs. Myriam Josza the President of the Sai Baba temple in Montreal, who had befriended the author during the Parliament of World Religions and Yoga in 1987, invited him to begin initiating the devotees of their society into Babaji's Kriya Yoga. Over the next two years he initiated more than one hundred of them in a series of nine weekly classes, with the blessings of both Sai Baba and Babaji Nagaraj. It is indeed rare that one spiritual tradition can be shared within the context of another. Too often, politics, fanaticism and ignorance deny the possibility. As described in the book *"Babaji"*, Yogiyar had been introduced to Babaji by Shirdi Sai Baba, thirty-eight years earlier. Now, Satya Sai Baba, had introduced the author and Babaji's Kriya Yoga to his devotees.

Yogiyar, in the meantime, immediately replied in a letter saying that he should stop initiating others. He even contacted the President of the Sai Baba temple, who is one of Sai Baba's closestdisciples, and tried, in vain, to get her to cancel the initiation classes. Yogiyar said that it was his Board of Directors who were to eventually decide where and when he would be allowed to initiate others. Further exchanges between them convince the author that Yogiyar has both a public and personal opinion on this issue. Yogiyar's longstanding need to keep a tight control on the students in his organization while enabling the author to teach independently underlies his public disagreement with the author; but personally, he accepts Master's decision to have His Kriya Yoga disseminated through the author.

Babaji's Kriya Yoga is shared with persons all over the world.

While the ways of the Master may appear to be mysterious, when seen from a limited perspective, the author believes that Master had a clear purpose in creating this situation. The Kriya Yoga tradition is like a great tree, whose trunk is Babaji himself, whose roots are the 18

Siddhas and whose branches include the many current teachers and organizations of Kriya Yoga around the world. While each of the organizations currently involved in teaching Kriya Yoga is doing wonderful work, each had developed serious limitations. There was a need for another vehicle for His teachings and those of the 18 Siddhas: one that would help many aspirants around the world to integrate their spiritual and material lives. The world is filled with religions and renunciant paths which lead persons away from the world, either to heaven or to liberation from the cycle of birth and rebirth. What is needed is not a new organization, nor a new religion nor a new belief system. Nor is Babaji seeking to establish a cult of personality centered on Himself. What is needed is for many thousands of persons to dedicate themselves to the transformation of themselves and of this material plane of existence. Through the practice Babaji's Kriya Yoga in the context of their worldly challenges a growing spiritual consciousness can be brought to bear upon the problems of human nature and material existence. Eventually, when the preparation is complete, a divine consciousness may descend into all of humanity, bringing about a heaven on earth.

In April 1991, the book *"Babaji and the 18 Siddha Kriya Yoga Tradition"* was completed and published by the author in English and French. Readers from around the world began responding. Since late 1991, Babaji has sent the author and his wife Gaetanne Annai to give initiation into His Kriya Yoga to about 3,000 sincere persons in more than 40 cities in 11 countries. Many lives were transformed. In 1992, they founded "Babaji's Kriya Yoga Ashram" in St. Etienne de Bolton, Quebec on a beautiful 40 acre mountain top estate near Montreal. Here they have organized year round activities, including retreats, summer camps and initiations. Annai Govindan, the author's wife, studied "ayurveda", the Indian wholistic health system in Aluva, Kerala, and developed at the ashram a wonderful facility for ayurvedic treatments, rejuvenation and inner cleansing, known as "pancha karma". The author's students around the world have formed meditation circles and regularly meet and practice together in one another's homes. In 1993 he published the first English translation of *"Thirumandiram: A Classic of Yoga and Tantra"* by Siddha Thirumoolar, which the Yoga Journal has called in a recent review "as important a yoga scripture as the Bhagavad Gita, the Yoga Sutra, or the voluminous and inspiring Yoga Vasishtha". In 1995 and 1996 the book *"Babaji and the 18 Siddha Kriya Yoga Tradition"* was translated into into Italian, Russian, German, Japanese, Spanish and Telegu. The author is currently involved in teaching in many new places, publishing a quarterly "Journal of Babaji's Kriya Yoga", in developing the activities of the Quebec ashram, and in the nurturing of a new "Order of Acharyas of Babaji's Kriya Yoga", a fraternal order of teachers dedicated to spreading the fragrance of Babaji's Kriya Yoga to all corners of the globe.

How I became a disciple of Babaji?

It has been a gradual process of completely surrendering the ego to Babaji thoughout the above described events and trials. By sincerely following Babaji's teachings, practicing His Kriya Yoga incessantly, cultivating love and devotion for Him, attuning to Him through his complete surrender mantra and serving Him and His mission to bring His Kriya Yoga to devotees all over the world, the author became Babaji's disciple. Many persons feel devotion for Babaji, but few choose to let go of the ego-bound preferences needed of a "disciple", one who follows a prescribed discipline or "sadhana". Through the discipline of Babaji's Kriya Yoga, one is transformed. The "ego", the habit of identifying with the thoughts and feelings is gradually surrendered: all expectations, desires and fears are detached from, and what remains is effulgent and continuous self awareness.

For further information on Babaji's Kriya Yoga, its publications and tapes contact:

BABAJI'S KRIYA YOGA AND PUBLICATIONS, INC.
196 Mountain Road, P.O. Box 90
Eastman, Quebec, J0E 1P0
Canada

Telephone: (514) 297-0258, or 1-888-252-9642
Fax: (514) 297-3957

Internet: www.iconn.ca/babaji/
E-mail: babaji@generation.net

- Cap-Saint-Ignace
- Sainte-Marie (Beauce)
  Québec, Canada
  1997